Building Your Professional Profile

How to Enhance Your Career and Win Business

Author
Rebecca Harding

Managing director
Sian O'Neill

Building Your Professional Profile: How to Enhance Your Career and Win Business
is published by

Globe Law and Business Ltd
3 Mylor Close
Horsell
Woking
Surrey GU21 4DD
United Kingdom
Tel: +44 20 3745 4770
www.globelawandbusiness.com

Printed and bound in Great Britain by Ashford Colour Press Ltd.

Building Your Professional Profile: How to Enhance Your Career and Win Business

ISBN 9781787423541
EPUB ISBN 9781787423558
Adobe PDF ISBN 9781787423565
Mobi ISBN 9781787423572

Table of contents

I. Introduction

1. Why do we need to take control of our professional profile?
Every day, we receive information about professionals, companies and organisations and what they can do for us. This information helps us to understand them and form an opinion about their work. We can also easily find out what sort of reputation they have.

With so much information available, it is essential to know what is out there about you. People will no longer engage you simply on the strength of a referral alone; they will look elsewhere to see whether you have a good reputation and whether you seem like the type of person they want to work with.

Taking control of the information that is available about you is an important first step. However, this also presents you with an opportunity to take the next step and actively manage your reputation. Most lawyers are not doing this; so there is a clear opportunity for those who do to become much better known.

However, as we know, there is a huge amount of information clutter out there; so how do we stand out in the marketplace? This is exactly why top businesspeople proactively manage their personal brands. They control messages about themselves clearly, as well as promoting themselves regularly through various media. This works for them, so it can work for you. Building your professional profile can dramatically enhance your career, help you to win work and ensure that you are presented with more career and business opportunities. It opens doors.

The other aspect to bear in mind is that in recent years, opportunities for lunches, events and traditional networking have significantly decreased. The number of clients attending events, for example, had diminished drastically even prior to COVID-19. We therefore need to look at other ways to initiate contact with new people. Fortunately, digital can give us a helping hand here: promoting yourself online can allow you to meet new people and show them who you are. As all professionals know, people buy people. At the end of the day, we are expected to have the technical expertise and know what we are doing as a baseline. Potential clients want to choose a lawyer who they have something in common with and who they feel they can work with. Building your profile and showing them your characteristics will allow you to attract potential clients who can identify with you.

"Potential clients want to choose a lawyer who they have something in common with and who they feel they can work with."

Building your profile will help you when trying to achieve certain goals – for example:

- building a professional profile to win work;
- becoming a partner or gaining promotion;
- moving firms;
- opening up more business opportunities;
- enhancing your credibility in the marketplace; or
- building your reputation with colleagues or clients.

"Taking control of my profile was one of the best things I ever did professionally. It has opened up so many doors for me because I think about the opportunities that I might be able to get for myself rather than just sitting and waiting for something good to happen. At first, it felt somewhat uncomfortable, as I wasn't used to putting myself forward. But I got used to it and realised that all businesspeople do it. Now I look for the opportunities without even thinking."

2. How will this Special Report help me?

This Special Report aims to help you develop your own professional profile. By the end, you should have a good idea about where you are going and what you need to do. It takes a practical approach to building your profile: you will learn about the process of communications, the psychological techniques that can help you and the practical steps which will dramatically enhance your public profile. Throughout the report, there are tasks assigned. These will help you to refine your thinking as you go along, until you have put together your own profile plan to take away and implement.

You may find that you have more experience in some areas than in others; so certain sections may seem obvious to you, while others may be completely new. But it's still worth reading the report in its entirety, as you may pick up new ideas or tips along the way; this will also help to link the content for you, so that it all makes sense.

As part of the process, we will also look at real-life examples. The report includes feedback from professionals and clients from a range of countries, including the United Kingdom. Some have attended courses on building their profile, and some quotes have been taken from these sessions and the feedback afterwards. All quotes were anonymised, so that individuals could be open about their experiences.

"I have always tried to build my profile, but I inevitably get distracted. It's my own fault that I've never got anywhere – I never bothered to put the time in and, to be honest, I never knew how to go about it properly."

II. Your personal brand

1. Getting started

Most people find it rather strange to think about their own personal brand. However, this is something that we all need to get used to, particularly in the modern digital landscape.

A 'brand' is defined as a particular "identity or image regarded as an asset".[1] Brands in business are regarded as extremely valuable and brand assets can constitute up to 80% of the value of a business. In recent years, everyone from actors to vloggers and reality TV stars have realised the value of individual brands. They have all built their own brands to commercialise who they are. They are essentially promoting the core elements of the person that they are – and making a lot of money in doing so.

Obviously, professionals have different objectives from actors and vloggers, but some of the key elements are the same. Let's start by thinking about why it is so important to develop your own brand.

When we think of famous businesspeople, we can see that they each have a defined brand of their own. This simply means that we have a very clear idea, from how they present themselves, about the type of person that they are, what they stand for and what they are about. From this image, we decide whether each person is someone we

"When we think of famous businesspeople, we can see that they each have a defined brand of their own. This simply means that we have a very clear idea, from how they present themselves, about the type of person that they are, what they stand for and what they are about."

would like to follow with interest – whether we will support their projects or listen to their viewpoints, or even try to replicate what has made them successful in their own lives.

For example, one famous businessperson might be very relaxed in how they dress, partake in physical adventures (demonstrating an entrepreneurial and daring spirit) and be highly positive in their approach. That person will attract people who want to be entrepreneurial and who aspire to those levels of daring and positivity.

If you look at the photos of famous businesspeople, the kinds of projects that they are involved in and the topics they choose to speak about, you will find that these are all consistent. Their reputations are often managed by media agents. This allows them to attract what is these days known as a 'tribe'. A tribe is a group of people with common values and beliefs. They find they can identify with that person's brand image: they can recognise the clear identifying factors, because these are consistent. They know what to expect from that person and, most importantly, they have an emotional response to them. They like them. They identify with their tribe and want to join it.

TASK 1A: Analyse the brand of someone famous

Choose a famous personality you like and answer the following questions:

- How do they present themselves in photos? What is their style?
- What clothing do they wear?
- How do they act?
- What topics do they speak or write about?
- Are these all consistent and in the same style?
- What qualities and characteristics do they display?
- What is their personal brand?

TASK 1B: Analyse someone well known in your marketplace

Is there someone well known operating in your own marketplace as competition? If so, conduct the same exercise on them and then answer the following questions:

- How and why are they building such a great profile?
- What can you learn from them? And what do you feel you could do better?
- How could you differentiate yourself from them in the marketplace?
- What makes you different and interesting?

2. What does this mean for us?

Just as famous and well-known people use techniques to promote themselves, so can you. If you understand what they are doing, you can do the same to build a professional profile. Your profile – your personal brand – can become as much of a valuable asset to you as their personal brand is to them.

"I love Richard Branson's personal brand. You always know exactly what you are going to get. Steve Jobs had a strong profile too, but very different from Branson's. It's interesting how they created very different images."

III. How do people choose their professionals?

1. The power of digital developments

Digital developments have completely overhauled how clients and potential clients look for information about professionals. In the past, they may have simply relied on a referral from a colleague and some information you provide about your experience. Today, however, they can also conduct their own research and will judge professionals based on their online presence.

According to research conducted by Forrester, potential clients gather information from at least three sources to confirm their decision to engage you as a professional.[2] A breakdown of the most important sources is as follows:[3]

- 30% like to hear you speak;
- 20% read blogs and articles you have written;
- 17% will have had some interaction with you on social media;
- 15% will have read a book that you've written;
- 8% think your website is good;
- 5% look at online reviews; and
- 5% do an online search.

This knowledge has changed how many professionals market themselves. You need to be sure that you feature in these different sources, and that the messages that they are giving about you are all consistent. It is worth doing a Google search on yourself to see what comes up. You may be surprised. The fundamental question is whether these online sources are presenting the right messages about you and the right image of you. If not, then it's time to take control.

"I needed to find a commercial lawyer in the UK and my legal contact sent me a choice of three. They did not want to commit to recommending one individual, so the choice was then left to me. I researched them and they all had the right expertise. I made my decision based on what I found. One seemed modern in their approach and interesting, so I chose that one."

2. You cannot afford not to engage online

It's no good saying that you do not participate online and that this is "just not something that you do" – although many professionals persist in this view. Hundreds of professionals are competing with you – and when prospective clients are looking for a professional, these others will stand out when those prospective clients conduct their own online research. The internet has made the market even more competitive than it was before, as people need not restrict themselves geographically when engaging professionals. With the use of digital platforms that facilitate internet conferencing, hiring professionals whom clients have never actually met, but have only come across online, is not just possible, but also increasingly common.

"I wanted to hire a divorce lawyer and, after I asked friends for some suggestions, I looked online to see how they all came across. I finally found a lawyer who I felt I could identify with. I liked how the website was presented and she looked relaxed and sympathetic. I liked the material she had written and her attitude. I spoke to her on the phone and met with her over the internet. I'm in the Midlands and she is in Brighton. I guess we might meet at some point, but to be honest it doesn't seem to be making much difference in terms of getting the work done."

IV. You are the business

1. Seeing yourself as a brand

Most people find it quite difficult to make the transition to seeing themselves as a brand. They are often self-conscious and may be uncomfortable about promoting themselves. The response to this emotional reaction is to think about the people you encounter at conferences, or as speakers and as writers. How do you think of them? Your perception of them is probably that they are smart, capable and interesting. You will not be actively questioning why they are promoting themselves in that way. The same goes for you. Nobody is going to think badly of you; they are more likely to be impressed.

"When I see great stuff done by my competition or if they are getting coverage, to be honest, I feel jealous. Is that bad of me?"

2. Promoting your profile

When it comes to promoting your own profile, you need to take a step back and think of yourself in the same way as your own firm's brand. Try to be dispassionate and objective. Imagine that your profile is a separate entity from you.

"I am a shy person, but I knew that if I was going to get my new firm moving, I had to start promoting myself. I felt so uncomfortable at first. I was used to hiding behind a big firm brand and that always

gave me authority. I hadn't realised how much I took from that brand in terms of my own self-belief too. I had to start from scratch and create a brand for myself. I had to work out who I was and what I stood for."

TASK 2: What is my profile now?

First, you need to determine what kind of profile you have now. Referring back to Task 1, think about your own profile in the same way. Start by doing an internet search on your name. What comes up?

- How do you present yourself in photos? What is your style?
- What topics do you speak or write about?
- What clothing do you wear?
- How do you act?
- Are these all consistent and in the same style?
- What qualities and characteristics do you display?
- What is your personal brand at the moment?

3. Consolidating your thoughts

You may decide that you don't have a brand or that it's not consistent. You may be pleased with what you find or you may be disappointed

"When it comes to promoting your own profile, you need to take a step back and think of yourself in the same way as your own firm's brand. Try to be dispassionate and objective."

that you are coming over in completely the wrong way. You may not find very much at all! Whatever you decide and whatever you find, see this as a positive first step. Without understanding this, you cannot work out where you are going or how to get there. Things can only get better from here.

"Searching online was interesting, because I thought it would show up lots of information about my professional work, but instead my charity work was far more prominent. Ultimately, I think this is a good thing, as it shows the kind of person I am; but it made me realise that I need to do far more to demonstrate my day job as a professional."

"I was shocked when I searched my own name online. I always had my photo taken at networking events and I would usually have a glass of wine in hand. What this meant, though, was that every single photo of me online, apart from my work profile picture, was a photo of me drinking alcohol. It was a terrible image. The glass always looks so big in photos too. I have got to put it right and I insist on putting any glass down now."

"When I searched for myself, there was barely anything there. I had a look at a guy I see as my main competition and realised he has quite a lot online. I've got to get myself in gear."

"I have always been active politically and when I searched on myself, all my political actions were there. This could affect my work. I had never really thought about it before."

"I discovered that someone else has the same name as me and is working in the same sector. I'm going to have to do something to clarify the situation."

V. What do you want to achieve?

1. Identify your objectives

The first step is to be clear about what your objectives are from this process. These will depend on:

- your findings from your Google search on yourself and your competition;
- how you would like to be seen in the marketplace; and
- what you want to achieve in terms of your career and the opportunities you wish to open up for yourself.

2. Case studies: Alice and Matt

Let's look at two example sets of objectives. These are the real objectives for Alice, a partner in a firm in New Zealand, and give an overview of what she wanted to achieve:

- to increase her profile externally in order to draw in business;
- to establish herself as a key influencer and, as such, a commentator in the sector, with clear views and values;
- to increase awareness of her work areas and her experience; and
- to enhance her profile internally and create a positive example for her staff.

Let's look at another set of objectives. These are quite different as Matt – a partner in a medium-sized, regionally based firm – had other issues to tackle.

"I was appointed managing partner of my firm at the age of 32, which meant that I was working alongside some much older partners who doubted my abilities because of my age. I used profile building to establish my credibility with them as much as anything else. The better my profile became externally, the more my fellow partners saw me in a positive light and as an asset to the firm."

Matt's objectives were:

- to build his credibility as managing partner;
- to present himself as a capable managing partner through thought leadership;
- to establish authority in the media/IP sector;
- to attract new work; and
- to build credibility with partners opposed to his appointment.

"I had a terrible time with the new joint management team after our merger. I only gained more respect from the new guys when they saw me out and about representing the firm and bringing in work by raising my own profile."

TASK 3: Set your objectives

When thinking about objectives, ask yourself the following questions:

- What are your key priorities?
- Where do you want to be known?
- Who are your key audiences?
- Are there any problems that you can deal with through profile building (eg, becoming a partner, internal issues)?
- Are there any particular marketplaces in which you want to become better known?
- What do you want to happen as a result of profile building? Can it help with career progression?

By answering these questions, you should start to get a good feel for what your objectives are. Try to keep to five objectives at the most, so that you can remain focused. It is better to do a couple of things well than to try to do too much, particularly when starting out. Ultimately, you want to feel a sense of success, not a sense of failure – so be realistic.

VI. Who do you want to reach?

1. Identify your audience

The more specific you can be about who you want to reach, the more successful you are likely to be. It is far easier to get a message across to, or to build your profile with, a smaller audience: you can make a real impact. Being too general and trying to reach everyone is one of the most common problems seen in professional services.

For example, you may want to become known as a commentator on medical litigation in the dentistry market. This is clear and focused, and dictates the actions required. The narrower your target, the easier and quicker it is to make an impact.

> *"One firm in Newcastle that we were working with, when asked about the target market, said that they wanted to appeal to every business, in every sector in the whole of the Newcastle area. They were then asked whether there was a particular size of business they were interested in. They replied that they didn't want to rule anyone out and if they could win some big businesses, that would be great, although most of their clients were smaller. This brief was an impossible challenge, being far too wide to reach anyone with any impact."*

Two lawyers set up a small online firm in the Midlands. They thought carefully about who would get the most benefit from the digital relationship. They intended to conduct all their meetings over digital platforms (this was prior to COVID-19, so it was innovative); all accounts would be held in the cloud; and they would be available via their own app for questions and support. They decided that small retailers would benefit greatly from this set-up, as they often do not have the time to visit an office during working hours. Building time flexibility into the digital service allowed them to support small retailers. As a result, they were able to focus exclusively on the retail sector. The partners appeared in retail trade materials and at conferences. They spoke and wrote about the common issues for small retailers. They successfully built their profile and saw clients increase dramatically from this exposure.

Marketing yourself is no different from marketing your firm. However, your time commitment to it may face pressure, as you will probably have no support with these activities. Therefore, the clearer you can be in terms of who you wish to build your profile with, the more successful you are likely to be and the quicker you will start to see some tangible results.

"I had worked in a large firm for years on intellectual property. I finally decided to go it alone. I realised the best place to start was with marketing and advertising agencies, as they were the people who developed the ideas in the first place. I focused my efforts entirely on this sector. I would speak about practical, interesting and entertaining examples in the industry, run some free training sessions and write as much as I could about the sector for various websites and on social media. As I met more and more people, I started to see a real difference in the number of people that would come to me and the opportunities that people were offering me to write or speak. Ultimately, it generated work and I could see myself becoming better known. The more I did, the more I was seen. The more work I did, the better the examples, client names and case studies became. And more work came in as a result. It was a virtuous circle once I got going."

2. Think about your area of focus

It may be that your focus isn't on a particular industry sector, but rather on a discipline area. This can work successfully too, if you are entirely focused on it. Marc became a partner in a large firm and wanted to build his profile further in the restructuring, insolvency and turnaround area. He attended everything that was happening in this field and made a point of visiting all of the key players (eg, accountants, banks, private equity, turnaround business experts) on a regular basis. He wrote every week about issues that he encountered, as well as running webinars and speaking wherever

"The clearer you can be in terms of who you wish to build your profile with, the more successful you are likely to be and the quicker you will start to see some tangible results."

possible. He would send interesting articles and information to targets. His social media presence was excellent and, importantly, consistent.

Let's look again at Alice. Alice works in intellectual property, so marketing agencies and staff are a key target for her. Alice defined her targets as:

- marketing industry leaders;
- marketing teams;
- chief marketing officers;
- her own team; and
- fellow partners.

"It has been quite enlightening to think about targets like this. I always work on the hope that anyone might give me work. But I know in reality that isn't true. It makes it impossible to know where to start."

"I have had so many ideas about other people who may want my expertise. I can't believe I got stuck in a rut like this."

TASK 4: Who is your target audience?

Carefully consider your target audience:

- Do you want to reach one or more trade groups?
- Do you want to reach technical experts in a certain field?
- Where is the most interest likely to be in what you do?
- How easy will it be to reach that group? Is this realistic?
- Who are the key people you need to reach within that group?
- Are there any other groups you need to target (eg, other partners)?
- Are there any other influencers in this field who you may not have previously considered?
- Are there other markets that could use your expertise and could become your primary focus – perhaps where there is less competition?

VII. Who are you?

1. Your USP

Now we will look at how you want to come across and what you want to be known for. This is the same as the USP or differentiator of a business. In other words, what is special about you that makes you stand out from everyone else?

It is important to be honest about your own qualities, both positive and negative. Most lawyers find recognising their positive qualities the most difficult part! It may be worth talking to a colleague about how you come across and what they see as your strengths. Then ask them to help you address your weaknesses. How could you improve your image? Do they think you could come across better if you changed certain aspects of your self-presentation? Importantly, present yourself in a good light, but as honestly as possible. For example, there is no point in trying to pretend that you are humorous if that is not something you are naturally.

> *"I was surprised when I asked my team how I came across to other people. It was quite different from how I saw myself. It's funny how you have one thing in your head and everyone else sees something else."*

The other point to keep in mind is that a certain image may help to attract certain types of clients in the marketplace. It is important to think about how your personal image will impact on potential clients. What will appeal to them? Try to integrate your personal image with some of the qualities that you think they will be looking for too.

Let's take a look at Alice's section on her plan.

1.1. Who is Alice?

- Strong personality
- Funny and entertaining
- Has strong, provocative and creative points of view
- Empathetic
- Loves her industry
- Is passionate about people and training people
- High energy
- Determined

Every time Alice undertakes an activity or produces material to increase her profile, she ensures that it reflects these qualities. She checks that any activity she undertakes is in line with her objectives and does not contradict them or take her off on a tangent. This approach is important to keep you focused on those activities which will reinforce what you are trying to achieve and ultimately to ensure that you achieve your objectives.

"It is important to think about how your personal image will impact on potential clients. What will appeal to them?"

TASK 5: Who are you?
In this task, you will look at establishing your USP:

- How do you currently come across?
- How are you currently known?
- What are your strong qualities?
- What could you present better about yourself?
- What image would help to position you in the marketplace? What did your current clients like about how you came across? (Ask them!)
- Going back to the successful profile of someone who is your competition in Task 1b, how can you differentiate yourself from them? How can you be different from others and interesting to potential clients?

By answering these questions, you should now have a list of qualities like Alice's above.

2. Tone

Tone is all about your 'voice' – the 'way' you write materials or 'how' you speak. For example, here is how Alice defined her tone:

- Positive and happy
- Humorous
- Empathetic
- Challenging, creative and fun
- Innovative thinking
- Experienced and seen it all before
- Competent and expert
- Relaxed
- Honest and straightforward
- Plain speaking to business people. No jargon
- Down to earth, with practical ideas and examples

These all complement the unique characteristics that Alice identified in the previous chapter and help to inform the types of material that she produces. For example, Alice has a smallholding as well as being a partner in a law firm. She decided to write a diary where she compared activities on her farm with those at work. It was humorous and entertaining. It allowed her to express her tone and the characteristics listed above. Importantly, it attracted attention in the marketplace. She became a 'personality'.

"I wanted to be genuinely different in the marketplace and it was hard to find a way to do it within the professional sphere. Everyone was talking about their technical excellence, their professionalism or their trade expertise. I decided to take a completely different

approach. I decided to take a stand on animal testing and help animal charities. I supported national and local associations and established partnerships with businesses that focused primarily on animal cruelty, such as make-up companies. I became an active speaker, talking about how we can help make a difference. I attracted a lot of new work to the firm from people who were animal fans. They respected what I was doing in this area."

TASK 6: Find your voice

To identify your own tone, answer the following questions:

- What kind of language will you use?
- Are you relaxed or formal?
- Are you straight talking or intellectual?
- Are you highly technical and specialist or practical and generalist?
- Are you serious or entertaining?
- Are you original and cutting edge or traditional and dependable?
- Does this style suit your marketplace and the potential clients that you are trying to reach?

Refer back to your answers to these questions before producing any written materials or social media posts. Remind yourself who you are and how you speak. Consistency is the key if you want to build your profile successfully.

"Thinking about my tone has helped me to write more confidently. SMEs do not want jargon and technical language. I have developed my style and it seems to work with my clients and contacts. I look at my writing in a far more critical way now."

3. Key messages

Key messages define who you are and set you apart from the competition.

Messages are the key points that you want to make to your audience. What do you want them to learn from you? What do you want them to think of you? These key messages will dovetail with your objectives. Your key messages need to feature in everything you do. However, you do not need to refer to them all the time. You simply need to demonstrate them. For example, if you want people to understand that you have a highly innovative approach to problems within a sector, you should write on issues or problems – and solutions – that demonstrate this innovative approach.

If a post, article or other opportunity does not fit with your key messages or objectives, you need to question why you are doing it or whether it can be changed to incorporate these. Can it be made more relevant to your purposes? Judging whether opportunities are relevant to your key messages and objectives is a good way of working out where to spend your time. Be ruthless, to ensure that you achieve what you set out to do. It is very easy to get distracted and lose focus. With a limited amount of time available, focus is essential.

"I love the fact I can say 'no' finally. I decide whether something fits with my objectives and messages and if not, it's gone. It is freeing."

What were Alice's key messages?

- Alice's firm is fast moving and fast thinking. It has the energy of a start-up.
- Alice believes in provocation and having new points of view.
- Alice is a trusted adviser, giving valuable guidance on hot topics.
- She is open and transparent.
- She will help you to understand how to protect your business.
- She wants to be seen as part of your business and your internal team.
- She provides innovative solutions.

"Your key messages need to feature in everything you do. However, you do not need to refer to them all the time. You simply need to demonstrate them."

All of these points were important to Alice and were what she wanted people to think after interacting with her. She wanted to come across as business focused. She based all of her materials and activities around these statements, and ensured that everything she did demonstrated one or more of them.

TASK 7: Your key messages

In the first instance, aim for about five key messages. Answer the following questions to help work out what your key messages are:

- What do you want people to think about you?
- What do you want them to associate you with?
- What do you want them to learn about you?
- What kind of professional do you want them to think you are?
- What kind of team member are you?
- How do you work?
- What is your work style?
- What are you expert at?
- How can you contribute to their business or firm?
- Why are you different from the competition?

"Once I had it clear in my head what it was I wanted to say and demonstrate to people, I noticed that writing posts and articles and deciding what to do was so much easier. And I gradually noticed people starting to talk to me about those issues too. The message was getting across because I just kept repeating it."

VIII. Your approach

1. How do you interact with others?

Naturally, how you interact with other people can make a substantial difference in terms of the success of your relationships and ultimately your profile-building success. There are some general approaches that can help you to improve relationships and some psychological tools that can lead to the establishment of strong connections. The better your relationships with people, the more likely you are to be asked to take part in opportunities and activities that will enhance your profile. Obviously, it will help you win more work too.

2. Friends first, business second

Ensuring that people see you as a genuine person and as a colleague, or even as a friend, is effective in terms of establishing business relationships. We often keep people at a distance in business, in order to retain 'professionalism' or to protect our time. But this can be detrimental in terms of progressing relationships. You can still be professional and show warmth and kindness.

This progression can easily be achieved by spending time talking to individuals about their families, their careers, what they did at the weekend and so on, and looking for points of commonality and areas where you can support or encourage them. Spend time on them and be interested in them as individuals. The best way to promote yourself is to take time over others. You can also make gestures to help improve their career prospects or introduce them to other colleagues. This interest and generosity will build their trust in you and their loyalty to you.

When people feel loyal to you, they are more likely to involve you in projects and opportunities. When selecting someone to work with on a project, people always justify their decision with rational arguments and business reasoning. But the reality is that people make decisions based on their emotions.

Nobel Prize winner Daniel Kahneman's research on how people make decisions revealed that our brain has two distinct operating systems, which he called System 1 and System 2:[4]

- System 1, he said, is based on fast, instinctive, unconscious and emotional factors. It is generally thought to count for over 90% of all decision making.
- System 2 is based on deliberate logic and rational thinking, and accounts for a small proportion of all decisions made.

3. Tapping into the emotional decision-making process

In order to build a profile and open opportunities, we need to tap into that emotional decision-making process in others.

"I was able to introduce one client to another of my clients as I thought they would both benefit from the introduction. They decided to do business together and went out of their way to make sure that it involved me too. It was profitable for everyone and the success cemented our relationships."

"I knew that a business was desperate for help in a certain area and I knew a client who could help it. I managed the introduction carefully and my client won the work as a result. They were so pleased. I noticed a change in the relationship. It became much stronger and we are now a lot better friends, as well as still working together. He constantly tries to make introductions for me."

IX. On the couch: some useful psychology

Two psychological tools can help you to tap into the emotional decision-making process of others and can lead to a positive reaction for you.

1. Association

'Association' is where you put yourself together with other people who are highly credible professionally. By being seen with them, you are perceived as being associated with them. People understand that you are well connected and therefore competent. In their minds, you gain or share some of the other person's credibility too.

> *"I had the great opportunity of making a speech in one of the side rooms at the House of Lords as I was attending an event there. Afterwards, I took a picture of myself with the baroness who was attending. I later added some general pictures of the House of Lords. I posted it on LinkedIn saying that I'd made my first speech at the House of Lords, as a bit of fun! I got a lot of interest on LinkedIn because of this post. Lots of people contacted me to find out why I was there. It re-established some old relationships and opened up conversations with others, leading to meetings."*

2. Reciprocity

People feel instinctively indebted to you if you do something for them and ask for nothing in return. They will be driven by the need to return the favour in order to be polite. The other advantage of making yourself useful to a client, potential client or contact is that they will see how 'useful' you are as a colleague; as a result, you become valuable them. It also builds trust and loyalty, as discussed earlier.

"I met a new business contact and soon realised that a lot of my business network would be useful to her too. I made a number of introductions and got her through doors she had never expected to get through. She was so grateful – she gave me some of my biggest client jobs this year. She has also referred me to others as well. She's been so kind!"

"I offered to write an article for a legal website. The editor was so pleased that she made an introduction to a US organisation which produced legal podcasts. I was interviewed by them and that interview was sent out internationally. I had several enquiries about the subject matter and it was good to link the podcast to my LinkedIn profile; I sent it out widely on email too. Many of my current colleagues saw it and were impressed that I was doing interviews in the US. It raised my credibility in their eyes."

TASK 8: Friends and helpers

Make a list of business colleagues or contacts with whom you would like to build a new relationship or develop your existing relationship. For each, think about what you could do to help them. You could:

- send them regular pieces of information or articles that you think they might be interested in or would be helpful to them;
- introduce them to other contacts you have;
- invite them to an interesting event/Zoom;
- refer them for potential work;
- ask if you can quote them in an article that you are writing;
- share their social media posts and/or 'like' them;
- refer them as speakers or as guests for webinars or conferences with other people; or
- send them an interesting book.

"There was one contact I wanted to develop into a client. Every couple of weeks, I sent them a piece of information or an invitation, or pointed out something interesting to them. Finally, after six months, they gave me work because they remembered me – I was at the top of their mind."

X. Where to be seen

1. Choosing your channels

Once your target markets have been identified, you need to choose your channels. By 'channels', we mean the different ways of delivering your message to the client or potential client.

It is important to maximise the use of an idea you have (eg, an article on a particular subject) across as many relevant channels as possible:

- It maximises your time and impact; and
- It helps to emphasise the message through 'opportunities to see' (an advertising term). This means that the more times that somebody sees a message, the more likely they will be to take it in and remember it.

Channels can include those highlighted in the Forrester report and others, such as:

- online reviews;
- speaking opportunities;
- blogs and articles;
- vlogs (short video recordings of one to two minutes);
- interactions on social media;
- an e-book that you've written;

- online search materials (eg, profiles);
- websites and relevant news sites;
- courses and training;
- technical journals/websites;
- seminars/Zoom sessions;
- news, features and case studies;
- LinkedIn posts;
- email newsletters; and
- direct mailing of referrers.

"I decided to write an e-book about diversity because of my own ethnicity. I work with HR departments anyway and this e-book made a great gift to send to people. It also started conversations and built relationships; and I was asked to speak to various staff and other departments. I am glad I did it. I promoted it in lots of places and the take-up was good, as well as raising my profile and getting me new contacts."

2. Getting the most impact from your channels

The need for content is never ending and platforms are crying out for interesting material on topical issues. You can volunteer to provide it. Alternatively, ask directly if you could provide them with material and see what they are interested in. It is reasonably easy to get material distributed.

Material need not be as long or as technical as many professionals think. We always think that we need to go into lots of detail. But something quick, general and short, making a good point, is far more effective. It will get read and it will have an impact. Think about the types of articles you like to read yourself. People often scan quickly and want to take away one strong point. You need to grab their attention. Write as you wish to read – unless, of course, you are writing a specifically technical article, in which case more detail is required. Think about your audience carefully and who is looking at the channel you are using. You may need to adapt material slightly to fit different audiences and channels.

TASK 9: Channels for targets

For each of your target markets or groups that you want to reach, think about where you might find them. Then use the list of potential channels above as a guide to see which will be relevant for each of your audiences.

"I wasn't even beginning to reach my targets. I hadn't given a thought to all the different channels that I could use and was just sticking to an email every now and again."

XI. Tactics

In this chapter, we will look at the kinds of actions that you can use to implement your plan. All the basics should be in place now, so you can start developing actions to support your objectives and messaging. This is an area where you can afford to be creative, innovative and inventive. If you are not that way inclined, try brainstorming ideas with friends or looking at what people are doing in other sectors.

> *"I started to look around at what others were doing in other marketplaces – the kinds of things people were doing on Facebook and in magazines. It all gave me ideas and I adapted them to suit me and my target markets."*

1. Social media

A large number of people have no idea why they use social media. They feel that they need to have a presence, but are not exactly sure why or what it is achieving for them. The trick with social media is to know who you are trying to reach and realise that it is a two-way media channel. There is no reason to be on every different type of social media platform if it is not relevant to your target audience. For instance, if we use the example of HR department staff, you are likely to find them on LinkedIn, but not on Twitter, as that is used more by journalists, creatives and politicians. If your target market is other lawyers – perhaps in-house lawyers – then you are most likely to find them on LinkedIn. You are unlikely to succeed in finding them on Facebook.

Let's have a look at the most common social media platforms.

1.1 LinkedIn

LinkedIn is probably the most powerful social media platform for business, but many people do not use it to its full potential. Most people in business and professional services have a LinkedIn profile. It is easy to do searches for different groups or types of specialisms. LinkedIn also makes suggestions for you of other potential contacts once it has worked out the types of people you are interested in connecting with. A good profile on LinkedIn will attract attention. If you see that someone has been looking at your profile, you can ask to connect with them and start a conversation. It is a great way to talk to and meet new people.

"I met my biggest client on LinkedIn. I asked to connect and he suggested that we meet. We got on well and realised that we had business contacts in common and had in fact worked in the same place in the past. He introduced me to others within his firm. As a result of this contact, I ended up with three international jobs too."

"I wasn't at all convinced by LinkedIn and its usefulness. But I thought I had nothing to lose by putting together a much better and more comprehensive profile. I was surprised to see how many more views I got and there was far more interest in me. I now need to follow up on these contacts and start to post regularly."

1.2 Facebook

Facebook is used by many consumer brands, as it promotes businesses and products to consumers. This is a more relaxed and social platform. It is also useful if you have a social or community programme at your firm and you want to promote it and engage with the community. In terms of professionals, it can be useful for reaching some groups. For example, a family lawyer may find Facebook useful in order to look approachable and access potential clients. Criminal barristers can also use Facebook now that the number of direct access clients is increasing.

1.3 YouTube

YouTube is a formidable search engine and is used to help people with everything from 'how to clean your kitchen work surface' to 'the food preferences of Hollywood stars'. In terms of business, a YouTube channel is a brilliant way to ensure that any webinars or interviews that you do will be seen again and again. Refer people to your YouTube channel, where they can see other things you have done, as well as the item you are referring to. You can also generate a link to use in a post on LinkedIn which will take people to your YouTube channel.

"We did a live webinar all about business turnaround and insolvency. We had about 40 participants on the day. We loaded the recording up to our YouTube channel and I was thrilled to see a couple of weeks later that we had had over 500 hits. We have had extra enquiries as a result."

1.4 Twitter

Twitter is fast moving and immediate. The sectors that seem to be most prevalent on Twitter are media, arts, education and politics. If these are the groups that you need to reach, then this is the place to be. Twitter allows you to make an instant response. For example, if you're on a live webinar, you can tweet immediately about it and get quick reactions.

1.5 Instagram

Instagram is consumer focused and picture driven, and has a younger target audience. If your market is young people or consumer-based companies (eg, pubs), then Instagram is a good place to be seen. For example, if you specialise in licensing, then Instagram could work well for you.

"Twitter allows you to make an instant response. For example, if you're on a live webinar, you can tweet immediately about it and get quick reactions."

"I specialise in the media sector and I dipped my toe in the water by getting on Instagram. I managed to connect with all the right people and it was surprisingly helpful in initiating conversations. Everyone was on there."

TASK 10: Which platforms?
Look at your target audiences and identify which social media platforms will reach them best.

If you find that you need to post on several social media channels, there are platforms available that allow you to post the same material on more than one channel at a time. These also schedule your posts for you. They can make life a lot easier.

2. Your own profile

On the whole, people are not particularly good at putting together their own profile. Modesty may get in the way; or you may find it too difficult to see yourself objectively. It is important to write something appropriate for an online profile, which can be used on your firm website, for your online profiles and even to go after an article put out in your name.

These profiles should all be consistent and effective. This is one of the most important aspects of who you are online. People will check them – particularly LinkedIn profiles – before they meet you or decide to instruct you. The photo that you choose is important. Think about whether the photo matches the image you want to portray.

"I'm an in-house lawyer and an external firm came to pitch to me. What they didn't realise was that I had actually worked there for some years and was a current alumnus. They hadn't bothered to research me properly. It was all there on my LinkedIn profile. I wasn't very impressed. If they hadn't bothered to do some basic research on me, then how thorough would they be on the job?"

2.1 Consider writing in the third person

If you find it very difficult to write about yourself and to objectively consider your attributes and skills, you may find it easier to write in the third person. The act of not writing 'I' and instead using 'she/he' can make it easier to give a positive commentary. It also makes better reading for someone else. It will come across as fact, rather than the very different impression that a first-person profile gives.

"I simply couldn't write my own profile because it just kept coming across as arrogant and it made me uncomfortable. I didn't want my own team to see it. By writing it in the third person, it came across in a completely different way. It sounded authoritative and factual. It

"If you find it very difficult to write about yourself and to objectively consider your attributes and skills, you may find it easier to write in the third person."

gave a much better impression of me and I could be more direct about my skills. I barely recognised myself."

When you start writing your online profile, go back to your USPs and your characteristics and messages. See how you can build these into your profile. In the 'About' section on your profile, you can give an overview of your skills. This is the place to build on your messages. For example, if you were in charge of an international job with a team, you could perhaps say that you have experience of international project management, diplomacy skills and an understanding of the cultures involved, and can be trusted with large-scale projects.

Obviously, you need to make sure that your profile is honest; but sometimes professionals underplay their skills to such an extent that it becomes detrimental when facing the competition. It may be worth getting someone else to write your profile for you, as they will be far more objective and likely to be more complimentary too. Don't forget, there's nothing wrong with selling yourself a little.

2.2 The impact of testimonials

Adding testimonials to the different sections of your LinkedIn profile is powerful. Many people leave the testimonials to the formal section allocated for this on the LinkedIn form, but few people read that far down. The section has also lost some credibility: some people recommend others for skills they do not have in order to receive a return recommendation, which has undermined the whole section.

A testimonial right at the start of the 'About' section is more useful. A sprinkling of testimonials throughout is even better. You could include a testimonial and a quote in each section of your LinkedIn profile and other online profiles. This adds to their authority: the combination of third person and external recommendations makes them more persuasive.

In terms of your photo, too many people use a personal photo on their online profiles. Instead, think about whether the photo is appropriate for the medium. Ensure that the photo presents your key messages, your tone and who you are, as defined earlier. If it doesn't, it's the wrong photo. The worst-case scenario is having no photo at all. Profiles without a photo are rarely read, as it appears that you are not active online. You don't come across as a human being.

Here is an example of the 'About' section on a LinkedIn profile for a barrister, written in the third person:

"It is always a pleasure to work with Joe. His case preparation is meticulous. He inspires clients' confidence with his thorough, strategic and pragmatic approach. He is a superb and persuasive advocate." Partner, Bloggs & Co

Joe Smith has nearly 30 years' experience as a criminal barrister, working for lay clients, solicitors and prosecuting authorities across the UK. He has become a specialist in white collar crime and fraud, and is a member of the Fraud Lawyers Association and the Fraud Forum. He is a valued professional on account of his unique approach to the people he works with:

- He believes in putting the time into listening to and talking to his lay clients. He will go the extra mile to ensure they understand and are involved in decisions. He works hard to embrace their position and concerns because his work affects their lives.
- He has a direct and clear communication style with clients, explaining issues simply and clearly.
- He employs a psychological approach and develops a holistic understanding of why someone has behaved in a particular way. What were the factors and what drove that behaviour? Sometimes clients do not make these connections themselves, but it can help their position.
- He is detailed and thorough in his approach. Experience has

taught him that you must turn every page and understand the entire brief to give the very best representation for the client.

- He is instinctive in his handling of highly complex situations and can facilitate negotiations to bring about resolution.
- He is outstanding at analysing the complex financial and operational problems that businesses experience in cases of white collar crime.
- He has an investigative approach to gathering and processing information, which enables him to advise clients quickly and strategically.
- He has the ability to establish good relationships at any level – after all, the relationship must be based on trust and mutual understanding.
- He recognises that it is crucial that clients have confidence in the representation they are receiving and goes above and beyond to ensure that he gives the best advice.
- He has worked in-house at a firm of solicitors, so he clearly recognises a law firm's needs as a client. He understands how to interact with firms and with their clients. He works on a collaborative basis and will work with all levels of staff at a firm to ensure the whole team is clear and on board with a case.

His areas of work are:

- fraud;
- serious violence;
- sexual offences;
- murder;
- kidnapping;
- robbery; and
- corruption and bribery.

"I couldn't believe the difference once I had worked on my profile. It was so much more interesting, attractive and professional. I could see how many more people were viewing my profile and were asking me to connect or interact."

"I changed my photo to one with a smile. Wish I'd done it years ago. Colleagues said I looked so much better and more approachable."

3. Titles

By title, we do not mean 'Mr', 'Ms' or even 'Sir'! Professional titles are hugely valuable in gaining recognition and getting people to respond to you. Quite simply, they make you more attractive professionally.

A professional title can be separate from your normal work area, but still be complementary and reach the right target groups. For example, you might become chairman of a specialist group at the Law Society. Alternatively, you can look at becoming a member of a group within the sphere of your target market. For example, if you're a family lawyer, you could join a specialist group looking at supporting children from split homes. Such a title gives you a credibility and status that your own firm title does not; you are seen as authoritative and high level. This perception will open doors for you. It also says that you are highly competent at what you do.

The fact of the matter is that the world is short of volunteers and if you are prepared to put in the time, there will be payback. Payback can take the form of open doors; access to thought leadership that you can pass on to your own contacts; current information to place you at the top of the game; association with, and introductions to, high-level contacts; and opportunities to speak and to write articles. As you are doing this on behalf of a society or an organisation, you'll be presented with the relevant title, but your work position and firm will naturally also get mentioned.

3.1 Professional titles = credibility

A title opens up a new world of credibility, and you will find that people will approach you wanting contact and connection.

"The advantage of working with a committee in a specific area is that it brings you into contact with exactly the right people."

"I am a commercial lawyer and I wanted to do more work in the motor trade, as I was building up a specialism. I discovered that one of the famous race tracks had a technology hub attached which was governed by a volunteer board. I offered to join this board and they were pleased to have me and my knowledge. I use my time to help them, but it also allows me to demonstrate my skills and to get to know the motor industry businesses in the hub. It has been hugely useful at opening opportunities, increasing my client network and improving my knowledge of the industry."

You might be reading this and thinking that such a role might be far too time consuming for you. However, you might want to think about the time you spend on fruitless networking events. The advantage of working with a committee in a specific area is that it brings you into contact with exactly the right people. So few people are prepared to volunteer that the door is wide open if you give your time and energy to an organisation.

"I work in criminal law and I often work for people with autism. I got involved with societies working in this area. It has improved my knowledge and capabilities when working with autistic people, and it has raised my profile as somebody who can help."

TASK 11: Where can you help?
Think about your target markets:

- What associations might they belong to?
- What organisations are they involved with?
- How about your technical area? What committees work on that? Can you join a relevant committee?
- Where could you volunteer? Write down some ideas and see how you can start to make contact with the chairman or secretary.
- Do you know anyone on the committee already?

4. Testimonials

We have touched on testimonials already and how effective they are in terms of impressing others and confirming your competence. They are far more believable than anything you will write yourself. Many professionals are shy of asking for them, but most clients or colleagues are more than happy to write something if asked – particularly if you're in a position to return the favour. The worst that can happen is that they say no; and if they do, it is probably for a political reason rather than anything else. If you feel comfortable enough to ask them, you probably have a good enough relationship with them. They are likely to say yes.

"Adding testimonials to my online profiles was a good move. I was surprised over the next couple of days that potential clients actually mentioned the testimonials and had read them. They clearly had a lot of impact."

TASK 12: Obtaining testimonials

It is not always easy to approach people for comments about your work and areas of competence. The following steps should help:

- Make a list of those people that you feel comfortable enough to ask for a testimonial.
- Write a list of work qualities that you would like the testimonials to highlight. Head back to the beginning and look at the qualities that you identified in Tasks 5, 6 and 7.
- Draft an email to those people individually. It could look something like this:

"Dear X, I am currently working on developing my online profiles. I am aware of the impact of a testimonial and the fact that it carries far more weight than anything I could write myself! I was wondering whether you could possibly write a testimonial for me to include in my profiles. I would be very grateful if you felt that this was appropriate. It would only need to be one or two lines long. There are a number of characteristics that are helpful in my work and that clients look for, and it would be useful if you could possibly refer to my abilities in these areas in your testimonial – if, of course, you felt that they were relevant. These are ...."

5. Awards

Awards, like testimonials, greatly enhance your profile. They are a great way to show your expertise and leadership in the marketplace. It is always surprising how few people apply for awards, mainly because the forms can be so onerous. If you have the stamina and the will to do battle with the forms, the likelihood of winning a prize can be quite high. On several occasions, business award ceremonies have shortlisted all of those that entered. Even being shortlisted for an award is a public display of your credibility and competence.

"We thought we would try to win prizes for a technical area, both for an individual partner and for the firm-wide practice as a whole. We were surprised at how easy it was to make the shortlist. We were even more surprised when we were told we had won both prizes! Our clients loved it and we were able to add it to the bottom of all our emails. It looked great; but more importantly, it has created some new business. It gave us a boost internally too."

TASK 13: Award yourself
Conduct online research into awards that you could apply for. Make a list and a note of the closing dates.

6. Building up followers

Even if you post the most innovative material, if you have no followers on social media, no one will see it. Connecting with people online is important in order to create new contacts and build up your following, so that more people are aware of your work area and what you do. The first 200 followers are always the hardest to win. After that, there is a snowball effect. You discover you have contacts in common, so people are more interested in connecting with you. Titles and awards also help to build trust in the connection process. It's worth spending five minutes a day, perhaps over lunch or coffee, connecting with new people on LinkedIn or other appropriate social media platforms. You can look to see who has viewed your profile and then offer to connect with them too. It is worth sending a message if people have reviewed your profile. You do not know what their interest in you was. It is worth finding out, as it may initiate a conversation.

It is also worth identifying those contacts you want to develop and drop them a line inviting them to meet for a coffee or to have a chat

"The first 200 followers are always the hardest to win. After that, there is a snowball effect. You discover you have contacts in common, so people are more interested in connecting with you."

through an online platform. The worst they can say is no. In reality, many will say yes, as they will want to extend their networks too. Look for a point of connection when contacting them – for example, having gone to the same university or having contacts in common – or tell them what interests you about their profile. Make it tailored and personal to them. You can also say that you want to expand your network – most people will understand that and be interested in doing the same. You can suggest to people that you might be able to introduce them to other contacts who would be valuable to them.

Look to connect with new people in your identified target markets. This is a great opportunity to make new contacts and you can use the search functions online to help you look for them.

> *"One of my biggest clients from last year came through LinkedIn. We simply agreed to meet for a coffee and to get to know each other, as we both realised we had worked at the same firm in London, although not at the same time. We got on well when we met and he thought in the same way about work. He introduced me to other colleagues and subsequently he and one of his colleagues gave me work."*

In order to connect, it is a good idea to like or comment on material people that other people are putting up. Professionals are always pleased when someone takes the time to do this and it can initiate a conversation on a topic that they are interested in. If you can keep the conversation going, you can then perhaps ask to chat on the telephone or via an internet platform, thereby developing the relationship.

> *"There was this lady who kept liking my posts, so I would always like hers back. Then we started to comment on each other's posts until finally, after six months, I suggested that we should have a chat over coffee. She thought it was a great idea."*

TASK 14: Think about followers
Plan a time each day when you will spend five minutes connecting with new followers and developing connections. Add it to your diary.

7. Putting a post together

The content of a post is important and should be thought through carefully. If your post is boring, too long or irrelevant, people won't read it and you might as well not spend your time on it. The purpose of a post is to get across a message. You need to present that message in a way that makes people interested enough to read it. This takes some imagination and thought. However, there are some basic guidelines that will help you to do this. So many posts are not interesting to anyone other than the people who wrote them.

"One of the most common mistakes you see is professionals putting in far too much technical detail and making their articles too long and unreadable."

7.1 The golden rules

There are some simple rules that will help you construct good social media posts:

- Is the post about the needs/problems of someone else? Why would someone else find it interesting?
- Do you have an interesting or unusual photograph?
- Does the post have an unusual angle on a topic?
- Can you film or interview someone? This would make it human interest and create association with your colleagues. Business colleagues will share the post if they appear in it, widening your audience and your potential to obtain new work.
- Is it short enough? People often write far too much; and if you feel you need to write a lot, this can put you off posting altogether. Keep it short and to the point. Ensure that every word has a reason for being there and is working hard.
- If you are writing an article about a technical topic, who is your audience? Specify the audience in your post. Remember who your target market is and what your objectives are, and craft your post so it is understood by the right people.
- Is it too technical for the audience? There is often far too much technical detail. Remember, you are not writing a contract or a technically dense document. You are writing to get over maybe

one or two points. One of the most common mistakes you see is professionals putting in far too much technical detail and making their articles too long and unreadable. This is a waste of time, as the target audience either won't read it or won't understand it. Either way, they won't take away the message.

7.2 Keep it relevant

Remember, people are in a hurry and want something that they can read quickly and easily. They do not have hours to sit reading lengthy documents. Think again about how you read. Make sure that your post is relevant and helpful to them, so that it is worth their while spending their time reading it.

- Do you have a good visual you can add in?
- Are you showing opinion and thus thought leadership through your post?
- Are you responding to a topical issue or raising a topical issue?
- Are you including any of your key messages in this post? How is the post working for you?
- Does the post present you in an appealing light? Would those reading it like to work with you and why? Is it showcasing what's different about you and your characteristics (as you identified earlier)?

"Think of hashtags as a way to connect social media content to a specific topic, event, theme or conversation."

If you ensure that all your posts are interesting and useful, people will remember that and search them out. You will attract more followers and raise your profile successfully. You will be remembered and your points/expertise will be taken on board.

"My most successful post ever was when I couldn't attend an award ceremony and so instead I sent my 14-year-old daughter with a work colleague. I was very lucky to win the award and my daughter was in all the photos receiving it. The post I wrote was not about winning the award, but about my daughter and how she got on in such an adult environment and how proud I was of her. This got more likes than anything else I have ever written. The photo was great and the caption was short. It caused a lot of interaction and correspondence with contacts, developing relationships. I became a human and they could relate to me. They saw me as a friend."

"I was talking to a contact who has a £40 million turnover international business. He said he had noticed my recent presence online and had liked the material I was generating. He asked me about some of it. He said it was good to see me there."

7.3 #hashtags

When you have finished your post, think about including a hashtag at the end. A hashtag is a word or phrase preceded by a hash sign (#), used on social media websites and applications – especially Twitter – to identify digital content on a specific topic.

Think of hashtags as a way to connect social media content to a specific topic, event, theme or conversation. They also make it easier to discover posts around those specific topics, because hashtags aggregate all social media content with that same hashtag. Essentially, they will help to attract an interested audience and people you have not had contact with before. There are websites that will help you to come up with ideas for hashtags and tell you what is 'trending'. Using popular hashtags will help you to expand your audience. Generally, you can run a couple of words together to create a hashtag – for example, #lawyerup #criminaldefence #businesslaw or #personalinjury.

However, one word of warning. Always be cautious before you publish and make sure to look for any potential misunderstandings or words that don't quite express what you mean. It is important to be realistic and think about how someone else might see or read your hashtag. This point is not to scare you off putting together a post; it's just to make you think about it from someone else's point of view and avoid misunderstandings.

"On National Women's Day, one partner decided to show how many women he had working with him in the office. He posted a photograph of himself standing with his arms crossed and his legs wide apart. He had three women on one side of him and three women on the other side of him. The women were leaning towards him and facing him, despite being partners or very senior. The image was terrible. It did not convey a firm of emancipated women. Rather, it conveyed a firm where women looked up to a dominant male figure who ruled the roost. Many people commented on it quietly behind the scenes in the city and it actually did more harm than good. When I mentioned the issue, I was told that I was being ridiculous."

Hashtags can also be a source of entertainment if not read objectively. Running a couple of words together can completely change the meaning, and there are many examples of professionals innocently creating a hashtag with a very rude or offensive meaning. For example, if you run the word 'experts' and 'exchange' together, it reads very differently indeed!

TASK 15: Post it
Have a go at creating a quick 'photo' post with a snappy caption. Try adding a hashtag too.

8. Social media policy

It's always worth checking before you start whether your firm has a social media policy. If you've usually sent out material through the marketing department, you may not have needed to know about this before – but there may be one. Ensure that you are aware of the policy if there is one, and understand what you can and cannot do.

"I was glad I checked the social media policy. There were a whole bunch of rules, but it was fairly easy to accommodate them and do what I needed to do too. They seemed mainly to be aimed at young people who might do crazy things."

XII. Seize the day

1. If you don't ask, you don't get

Don't be afraid to go out and create your own opportunities or roles. The old adage 'if you don't ask, you don't get' is so true. If it's a good idea, people very rarely say no; they usually wish that they'd thought of it themselves! Think about problems that your target market might have and how you could help to solve them. Could you perhaps start a new committee or work with a group on a special report to deal with a specific issue? Could you investigate it further? Who else could you involve? Think about what might be in it for them and why it would be a benefit for them to participate. This will help to encourage others to support you. Make it a win-win for everyone. It's important to be able to identify people's motivating drivers and priorities. Being the instigator puts you in the driving seat and establishes you as the expert.

"I had begun to learn more about whistleblowing and I came into contact with several cases. I realised that the law in the UK was different from the law in the US. There were opportunities to develop this practice area and to become known as an advocate for change. I found it easy to get speaking opportunities, to write articles and to put forward opinions. I received many invitations and it was easy to establish myself in this niche area."

"I wanted to establish myself as a commercial lawyer for SMEs in our region. I decided to put together a report on the key legal challenges for businesses in the region. I set up a committee to oversee it and invited all the local business groups to send a representative. I was chairman. It worked like a dream. The report got a lot of coverage in the press and with all the different business groups in their newsletters and so on."

2. Make the most of your personal and professional networks

As discussed earlier, introductions can also generate opportunities for yourself and others. It's important to be able to recognise the benefits for others and the potential business opportunities that you can open up if you introduce one of your contacts to another. If this prospective meeting is successful and creates business for them, they will often feel obliged to involve you in that or feel a need to make some reciprocal gesture to thank you. Most people are genuine and will reciprocate in some way.

The other advantage of introductions is that they establish you in the minds of those contacts as being in a leadership/influential position. You are seen as being associated with good professionals and as having an extensive network – as a door opener and a generator of business. You become a positive person to have around.

"It's important to be able to recognise the benefits for others and the potential business opportunities that you can open up if you introduce one of your contacts to another."

You can always ask your contacts for introductions too. They will know other people who would be good for you to meet, which will help to extend your network and influence.

"I decided to give it a go and asked everyone I met for a week to introduce me to a contact that they thought would be good for me to meet. Practically everybody did and it widened my network with some brilliant people."

It is possible to establish partnerships with complementary professions. For example, you might decide to do a joint presentation or webinar which would create a better, more exciting event, with broader content and wider appeal. This would allow all those involved to make new connections and extend their networks without directly competing. Again, this puts you in a leadership position, flatters another contact and opens doors for them. Speaking always makes you influential.

"As a commercial lawyer, I wanted to get into the motor trade, so we built a relationship with an engineering consultancy. There are many motor trade businesses in our area. We decided to do some joint events, joint help sheets and joint articles for the internet. It showed that we had in-depth knowledge of the industry; that we were well connected and well informed. We were able to combine our contact bases, which were complementary, and it proved advantageous for both organisations."

TASK 16: New people

Think about potential partnerships:

- Who would be good to partner with for your target market?
- Could you produce a report or create a new group?
- Who could you ask for introductions?

XIII. Ensuring that you are at the forefront

1. Think like a leader

How often do we hear people say that they are 'thought leaders' or 'at the forefront of their profession'? If you look at the definition of 'thought leadership' in the *Oxford English Dictionary*,[5] it refers to this as "intellectual influence; innovative or pioneering thinking". In 1994 Joel Kurtzman said that "a thought leader is recognised by peers, customers and industry experts as someone who deeply understands the business they are in, the needs of the customers and the broader marketplace in which they operate. They have distinctly original ideas, unique points of view and new insights".[6]

Putting forward different ideas or suggesting new approaches gets people talking about you – which is exactly what you want in order to build your profile. It is a good way to showcase and demonstrate your expertise without having to 'sell' it. Potential clients, current clients and other professionals will immediately see that you 'know your stuff".

But if we are honest, how often do we see such insight or original, innovative thinking demonstrated in practice? In fact, how often do we manage to do this ourselves? Thought leadership means expressing an opinion within your field which may be slightly controversial or alternative in its approach. For many professionals, this can feel somewhat uncomfortable.

2. Tactics for developing your ideas

How do we go about developing ideas that we can write about in order to present ourselves as thought leaders? Often we have thoughts that could be described as 'thought leadership' without realising it, because what we are thinking seems so obvious to us. But those ideas may not be as obvious to other people as they seem to you. It is worth keeping a notebook and jotting down ideas and thoughts as they occur to you. Starting to think about things in different ways is like exercising a new muscle: at first, it feels a little uncomfortable; but after a while, you get better at it. Once your mind starts to focus on these thoughts, you will find that they come faster and more frequently. Having your notebook with you or a file on your computer or phone is a great way to remind your brain to think about things. Why not set up a file or notebook dedicated entirely to ideas to do with building your profile? Then you can dip in and out of it for inspiration for posts, talks and webinars, as well as articles.

Reading articles, attending courses, listening to webinars, scanning LinkedIn, talking to clients and colleagues and chatting with other professionals or friends in other work areas are all ways to generate ideas and thoughts that can form the basis of articles and posts. If you examine what others are writing on a topic, you will see how they are setting out the same basic points over and over again. If you can come up with a different angle, you will show that you are original in your thinking.

Putting time into developing innovative ideas also helps when dealing with your clients, as they will be impressed with your originality. This time is never wasted; but so often, we treat reading and research as a necessary evil rather than a way to get ahead of the game. As well as helping you to develop ideas for building your profile, you may find that you start to have ideas about how to improve your service and what you offer clients too.

"Coming up with innovative ideas is hard. I found that talking to clients was the best place to get ideas – just listening to what their real problems were."

3. How can you ensure that your ideas stand out?

People look for information to help clarify a piece of legislation or a recent change in the marketplace so that they can better understand its impact and what it means for them. Articles that assist, advise and explain are useful; but often, all the articles that you see on the topic are exactly the same. How can you make your article different from all the others and make it stand out?

Think about how your article/post might be able to:

"Reading articles, attending courses, listening to webinars, scanning LinkedIn, talking to clients and colleagues and chatting with other professionals or friends in other work areas are all ways to generate ideas and thoughts that can form the basis of articles and posts."

- solve a problem;
- advise on a current point or legislation;
- promote a new idea or way of doing things;
- provide critical commentary on how things are currently done;
- pick up on something in the news/a topical issue and give an opinion;
- offer help sheets or explain a topic;
- demonstrate what you have learned from a recent piece of work; or
- share an entertaining anecdote with a message.

"I wrote a short article about inclusivity and laid out what I thought was holding firms back in this area. I put it out on social media and email, and I've had so many comments. It's allowed me to talk to people and develop relationships in a new way. In two cases it ended up bringing in some work. It also got me noticed internally and one of our senior partners contacted me to see if I wanted to look at introducing some of my ideas into our workplace. I was very pleased with all the feedback I got."

The next stage is to start to put together a plan around one of your innovative topic ideas.

For example, if you specialise in contracts for authors and other artists, then Twitter is a great place to be seen. You could look for writing associations and offer to run free hour-long webinar courses for members – for example, "How to ensure that your contract is fair and what to look for". You could also run a similar version, but somewhat amended, for publishing houses and literary agents. There are various websites for writers and trade magazines, so you could produce articles for those. There are trade fairs that normally take place, such as the London Book Fair and the Hay Festival, as well as a wide variety of other literary festivals. It may be possible to speak or present at them.

TASK 17: A great idea

Spend some time reading and looking at what other people are doing. Chat to some friendly clients. Can you generate one genuinely innovative idea? Try it out on colleagues.

XIV. Pick up your pen

1. The power of the written word

We briefly looked at articles and writing earlier, and here we look at this in more depth. Articles are a good way to establish recognition for your expertise and your professional work. These days, with the onslaught of digital platforms and the constant need for content, it is possible to get your work published in many different places if you are prepared to do it for free. Many editors are keen to find willing contributors who can write on current topics in an entertaining, original and engaging way. If you do a good job, they will come back to you again and again. And if you offer to do it again, they are unlikely to refuse you! You can also write more in-depth articles. Articles can be used on your firm website and as e-shots, posted online and circulated to other websites and platforms. If it is a 'news' idea, you can send it to a newspaper or news platform. Use your material in as many different places as you can. Once you've gone to the trouble of writing something, make sure that you maximise its value.

Once they have an idea, professionals tend to leap into writing densely technical articles. But the only time you should be writing technical articles is if your audience is also technical and is looking for a higher level of expertise. Otherwise, most articles are too long and not aimed at the right level for the intended target. Time is at a premium for everyone. If you think about how much material and information passes your desk and how little time you give it, you will work out how long you have to interest your reader. The bottom line is: you only have a few seconds to attract their attention at the beginning and entice them to read further. Think about the headlines and titles that catch your eye. What grabs your interest? Make sure that you write something that will have a similar impact on others.

2. Avoiding common pitfalls

Most of the material put out is of mixed quality and a lot of it is poor. A number of mistakes are commonly made. To avoid these mistakes, follow the guidelines set out below. If you do not have the time to write or know that writing is not your strong point, then find somebody who can ghost write for you – or perhaps even hire someone to do this if you have the budget. A professional writer can craft an article out of bullet points and a quick chat about the topic. They will often do background research to come up with more depth and angles for the article. This can be money well invested. If you are happy with the finished article, you can then distribute it as suggested above. Minimum work; maximum output.

All lawyers are now put under pressure by their firms to write articles and material for online content. One of the major problems with this is

"Many lawyers are not writers, so it takes them a long time to sit down and grapple with putting an article together. Procrastination is common, because they do not know what to say or how to say it."

that many lawyers are not writers, so it takes them a long time to sit down and grapple with putting an article together. Procrastination is common, because they do not know what to say or how to say it. They also have lots of fee-earning work to do, which must take precedence. They want everything to be perfect, but don't know how to achieve perfection in an article.

> *"My firm is always asking me to write articles and I can't stand it. I hate writing. I am not a writer. I don't know how to make it sound good. It always sounds dull and heavy going."*

Realising that an article need only be short can be very liberating. If an article is not short and to the point, it will not do its job. You will not get your point or your key messages across. It will not get read and – more importantly – it will not help to enhance your professional profile.

If getting professional help with writing articles is not possible, practise writing in a more journalistic style. Notice articles that you enjoy reading – whether online, in magazines or in newspapers – and see how they differ in style from the material that you produce yourself. The more you practise, the better you will get. Get other people to read and critique your work for you. It is much better if this is not another lawyer, but somebody who is a member of your target group or outside the area you are writing on. You will be able to see how much they understand and how engaging they find it.

> *"I signed up for an online writing course. It was only a couple of hours long, but it talked about how to write more like a journalist. It was useful and helped me to change my style. I look back at some of my old articles and they make me cringe."*

There is always the option not to write at all, but instead to dictate your article using the functions on your computer or your phone. This can help make your style more colloquial and improve your flow tremendously.

When writing articles and posts, think about the following:

- Who is your target market? How do you need to write to appeal to them?
- Will they be interested in the topic you have chosen?
- Is there an unusual hook in the article?
- Is it genuinely an innovative idea? What are others writing on this theme?
- Is every word in the article/post working hard? Or are there many words that you could easily edit out to make it shorter and punchier?

- Is the title interesting enough to grab someone's attention?
- Is it catering to the target's needs or just stating what you want to say? The target's needs should be the focus of the article.
- Have you made a clear point?
- Do the arguments follow logically for someone who does not know what you are talking about?
- Are you assuming understanding? Are you sure that the reader will understand everything that you have written?
- Is the language more complex than that used in a national newspaper? If so, it will probably be too difficult for the reader to read quickly and they will abandon it.
- Have you edited your work? Then edit it again! Make it shorter.
- If it has to be signed off by someone else, beware of the meddling pen and fight your corner. People are always tempted to add more in; but is it necessary?
- Do you have a visual image or photograph that you can use with the article? Even a picture of yourself makes it more human.
- Add a short sentence at the end describing who you are and how to contact you.

The article's purpose is to inform and entertain. If a reader is bored, they will not continue reading; the next article might be more interesting. If you are bored writing your article, you will not carry the reader with you.

"I had put together a short piece that I thought would be good to go out to the regional newspaper and publications. Sometimes these publications will just cut and paste the piece in. It had to be short and to the point, and require little editing. It was a new angle on a topic and I had come up with a hard-hitting headline. It then had to go to a senior partner for approval and he added in twice the number of words. It then had to go to someone else to be checked again. By the time it came back to me, I didn't even recognise it. It went from being half a page to nearly two pages. The likelihood of anyone using that was slim. The point was lost in detail and technical clarifications. They had completely forgotten that this was just aimed at the local newspaper and therefore didn't need to be very high-level. The journalists were not going to translate it before they printed it. It would end up in the bin."

The end result that you want to achieve is a reaction, recognition or comment from your audience and readers. This will allow you to engage with new contacts; or you may be asked to comment further on the topic. Providing a 'call to action' – such as a help sheet that you have prepared or a webinar on the topic that readers can attend – will drive them to engage with you further.

TASK 18: Pen to paper

Take the innovative idea that you came up with in the last task and write out a structure based on this idea for a short article – 500 words maximum. In your structure, think about your attention-grabbing opening lines, plan out the logical argument and think about an entertaining end. Then try writing the article. Check the list above and see whether you have followed the guidelines. What could you offer as an incentive to encourage readers to make contact with you?

XV. Time to speak up

1. Face your fears

At the beginning of this Special Report, we saw that one of the areas that scores highly for winning recognition with potential clients and encouraging them to work with you is public speaking. The very prospect strikes terror into the hearts of many people. However, this is something you can work on. And as the world becomes more digital, the opportunities to achieve the same effect via webinars and podcasts make the whole process far easier and less daunting if this is a skill that you are starting to develop.

"I was in charge of PR at a big international firm and they decided to put forward one of the quietest people I had ever come across to be the media spokesman for the press. I was extremely concerned about how this would work out. They wanted him because he was technically the best and everyone else was scared of getting something wrong. I put him through media training and he suddenly realised that he could get better at it, as it was a craft. He could learn it. He worked hard at developing the techniques and began to perform well. He became a media star on the radio and in the newspapers for the firm. This was because he understood what was wanted by an audience. He abandoned his technical skills and spoke as though he was talking to friends. He was easy to understand and got to the point quickly."

Your presence at the front of a room can have a distinct psychological effect on others. You will often see a queue of people waiting to engage with the speaker at a conference. The speaker is seen as being elevated in terms of the other attendees – it is rather like being 'famous for five minutes'. Make the most of this effect. It is the same on webinars and podcasts. This is why it's worth developing your technique. There are many courses that will help you with public speaking and presentations.

2. Maximising opportunities

Where do speaking opportunities come from? Good speakers are in short supply; as are speakers with engaging, new topics. If you can show yourself to be one or the other – or even better, both – you are sure to find new opportunities. If you have defined your target markets well at the start of this report, it will be obvious to you where you should be speaking and to whom you should be speaking. This will help you to identify the topics to focus on.

People will always be more eager to use you as a speaker/leader for a webinar if you are prepared to do this for free. Many are not and there is always a need for speakers that is not fulfilled. As we become more digital, there is a greater need for content and for people who are prepared to put their heads above the parapet. Seize the opportunity. Get out there and let people know that you are prepared to do it.

Here, we will briefly look at creating content. Once again, we need to think about a number of key factors, to ensure that we exploit this opportunity as best we can.

Here are some tips for generating and engaging in speaking opportunities:

- Use your own firm to host events or webinars where you are the key speaker.
- Use material from your posts and articles to create presentations/webinars. You will be able to see the material that has generated the most interest.
- Create a presentation that you can offer to other organisations, such as trade bodies. You can easily adapt it for a new audience.
- Do a joint presentation with another professional firm to enhance your contact list.
- Ensure that you think about your target audience and ensure that it is at the right level of understanding.
- Offer to present at trade and technical events (online if necessary).
- Ensure that you clearly present your contact details and where you can be found.

"Good speakers are in short supply; as are speakers with engaging, new topics. If you can show yourself to be one or the other – or even better, both – you are sure to find new opportunities."

- Is there a giveaway that you can offer people if they connect with you on LinkedIn or email you directly (eg, an electronic help sheet)?
- If you run a webinar, ensure that you contact everyone who attended. Immediately after the webinar, everyone will feel warm towards you as the expert – this is the time to capitalise on your efforts.
- Be adventurous in terms of trying new media. Podcasts are a great way to communicate and are easy for people to listen to on the way home from work or in the car.
- Try speaking on topics that are outside your normal work area, but that you have experience of. This sometimes open doors that your normal work would not. When lots of people are competing for the same contacts, being different is essential.

"We ran a good webinar for a partner who is trying to win work and improve his profile, as he is new. We had all worked hard to make it original and interesting. It went well and there were numerous comments in the chat box during the event saying how good it was. We sent the list of hot leads to the partner afterwards. Two weeks later, I rang him to see how he had got on. He told me he had not had time to ring and that he was going to try doing it now. I was disappointed. I knew the moment to cement those

relationships had gone, but the partner just didn't seem to understand that it was too late now."

"Although it's not my area at all, I got involved with a fraud case. I don't mean that I committed a fraud! I just came across one in my work and I ended up reporting it. It was a long, complicated story, which showed problems in the system and how difficult it was to get anything done in such a situation. Another lawyer suggested that I could talk about my experiences to a group that was interested in fraud. They contacted me and I spoke at their national conference. I simply told the story of what had happened and then commented on the problems in the system. Many people contacted me and came to speak to me afterwards. People felt they knew me and felt empathy with me because of what I had experienced. As a result of these new contacts, I won new work. I stood out. It opened up a completely new network for me."

TASK 19: Be heard

Look back over the list of ideas for webinars and presentations. Think about your target market or markets and see what topics, issues or ideas you have which would make good event material.

Once you have come up with some ideas, think about how you can make them different. Can you take a different angle? Are they aimed at, and of interest to, your target audience? Will they grab their attention?

Finally, think about the most appropriate medium. For example, would those ideas make a good podcast, webinar or course? Should it be just you or you and a guest? Do you need an interviewer?

XVI. Productise yourself

1. Turning your ideas into products

If you have good, innovative ideas – or even practical, common-sense ideas – these topics can be turned into products.

Products can take many forms, but essentially mean that your target has to engage with you at a higher level. They have to request interaction and, by doing so, they enable you to capture information about them and their interests. Products enhance your profile by adding another level of professionalism. Targets are impressed by products, particularly e-books and published books.

> *"I am amazed to have three books published now and it has definitely affected my prestige and credibility with clients. I give potential clients copies when I meet them and it makes a great impression. They are always pleased to get a gift."*

What kinds of products do we mean? These could include:

- e-books;
- self-published and published books;
- guides;
- help sheets;
- recorded courses online (easy to do with conferencing platforms, as they have record functions); and
- podcasts.

The options are endless, but the point is that you are taking an idea, showcasing your expertise and your key messages, and building your profile through the product.

Ensure that you include all your contact information, so that people can get hold of you, and details of your background. You want contacts to keep the product at hand and build a closer relationship with you through it. They will begin to feel that they know you and that they can easily get hold of you. You will be the first at hand when they do need you.

For example, a family lawyer could produce a Preparing for Divorce workbook. This could include advice, an action list, lists of information to get together, budget plans, an expenses planner, advice about dealing with fees, and sections about thoughts and feelings. It could include information about groups that provide support; and sections that readers fill in themselves, so that they use it regularly as an aid. Such a practical workbook could be a great support and could be given out free to potential clients; they would feel that you were already their lawyer before they even hired you. This would be a good item to produce with a 'partner' – potentially a professional who specialises in relationship breakdown support.

TASK 20: The product

- What could you produce as a product? You might choose one of the ideas listed above or you might think of something else.
- How will it help your target market?
- Why would someone want it or want to keep it?
- How will it demonstrate your expertise?
- How easily can you produce it and what might the likely costs be? Is it realistic for you or could it take another form?

2. Your internal profile

Building your external profile can help greatly with improving your internal profile. Your colleagues will notice your success, which can help with promotions or encourage others to include you in new projects.

"I was really struggling with my partners. One of them was trying to replace me in my role and I felt that I was gradually being pushed out. He wanted some of my responsibilities; it was not a nice time at work and I was stressed. I'd been working hard at increasing my external profile and found that I was starting to see some real success. I made sure I publicised this internally and by connecting on LinkedIn with my colleagues, so they could see what I was up to. I'm sure this is what made the difference. In the end, he didn't get what he wanted."

TASK 21: Reaching your team

- What actions can you take to ensure that your internal team see what you are doing?
- Are there particular people you need to reach? How might you do so?
- Are there actions that you can take to raise your profile that could be aimed internally?

3. Be committed

The biggest problem in professional services is a lack of implementation of plans and strategies. Strategies are developed, ideas are put down – but at the end of the day, everyone goes back to their client work. If you want this to work for you, you will have to commit to implementation – even if that means just five minutes each day. It is best to do one or two things on a regular basis than a lot every two years. If you can do it daily, that is the best.

"As a professional services consultant, I gave three different lawyers in the same marketplace an idea for a cutting-edge opportunity. They could all see how good it was and got very excited. However, none of them got round to implementing it. In the end, I saw another firm had done a version of it and they made the money."

"The desire for professionalism puts pressure on us to be perfect. The fact is we are not. We have to face that and just be happy to have a go and do the best we can."

Some professionals experience a lack of confidence, fear of failure or imposter syndrome when engaging in the new area of profile building. The desire for professionalism puts pressure on us to be perfect. The fact is we are not. We have to face that and just be happy to have a go and do the best we can. If you feel any of these things, just remember that you have nothing to lose. Something is better than nothing.

"I am a terrible procrastinator with things like this. I am so worried about making it all perfect that I can't seem to get started at all. I put it off day after day after day. But when I finally have to do it, it is never as bad as I think it is going to be. I know I am going to procrastinate over this because it makes me feel self-conscious. And of course, I have not done it before."

TASK 22: Barriers

Make a list of the barriers for you in building your profile:

- How will you deal with these?
- Are there training needs you have noted (eg, writing skills)?

XVII. Put together your plan

1. Choose your layout

In order to ensure that you implement your plan, it's a good idea to have it listed as a set of actions with a timescale that works for you. A spreadsheet or table is a great way to present it and lay it out for yourself. We are going to work on something that gives you more structure and commits you to completing tasks each month. This will allow you to achieve your overall objectives.

Overleaf is an example of a plan used by another partner. You will see that the types of activities are listed on the left. These are the activities that will enable the partner to achieve his objectives. Across the top are the months of the year. In each box on the spreadsheet there is a cross, indicating activity in that area of work. The idea is that if you ensure that you complete each of the crosses, you should achieve your overall objectives by the end of the year.

Figure 1: Example plan

Activity	Sept	Oct	Nov	Dec	Jan	Feb	March	April	May	June	July	Aug
Contacts												
Build up contacts on LinkedIn	×	×	×	×	×	×	×	×	×	×	×	×
Look for people to do joint presentations with	×	×	×	×	×	×	×	×	×	×	×	×
Make two introductions per month. Act as a broker between people	×	×	×	×	×	×	×	×	×	×	×	×
Attend awards, events and networking meetings twice a month	×	×	×	×	×	×	×	×	×	×	×	×
Digital												
Post at least twice a week on Twitter, LinkedIn etc	×	×	×	×	×	×	×	×	×	×	×	×
Rewrite your LinkedIn profile. Use on other digital media	×											
Obtain personal testimonials	×	×										
Film activities and post												
Connect with other internal people	×	×	×	×	×	×	×	×	×	×	×	×
Meet or discuss mutual promotion opportunities with internal contacts to build relationships	×	×	×	×	×	×	×	×	×	×	×	×
Speaking												
Develop speaking pack 1		×	×									
Develop speaking pack 2				×	×							
Identify organisations/conferences to speak at and approach them		×	×	×	×	×	×	×	×	×	×	×
Explore the idea of a mini conference	×											
Use ** as a platform to speak to clients and allow them to network with each other		×										
Titles and influence												
Make a list of key associations to target	×											
List potential personal awards to apply for and apply accordingly		×										
PR												
Identify articles for distribution		×	×	×	×	×	×	×	×	×	×	×
Develop a list of journalists in the trade, business and mainstream press					×							
Set up meetings and meet journalists					×	×	×	×	×	×	×	×
Product												
Produce a personal booklet/guide; this demonstrates expertise and can be given as a gift						×	×	×				

TASK 23: Your plan

Now you can create your own plan. This could be laid out on a spreadsheet, in a table or in any other format that appeals to you. However, it must include the work areas, the months and a spread of work over that time that ensures you have covered everything.

There is an example table overleaf that you can copy and fill in. You can print it off and use it to adapt and create your own.

Refer back to the notes you have made while reading this Special Report and add them into your table. You can add more or less as you wish, depending on how specific your ideas have been.

2. How to make it work for you

Often, people manage their initial plan, but then fall by the wayside in terms of its implementation. Sometimes this is because of time pressures; sometimes this is because they do not believe that the plan will work; and sometimes this is because they find the initial implementation hard work and slow to yield results, and begin to lose faith. However, if you do nothing, you will never get anywhere at all. Others will attack this and get better at it, leaving you behind.

Remember, this is your plan and you can keep it to yourself if you want to. No one needs to know about it and they will not know if it does not go the way you planned. But they will notice if it goes right!

If you are worried about the time involved in implementing your plan, there are a number of options to make it work for you.

First, if necessary, you can cut down on the amount in your plan and focus on one area alone. By being specific, you can reduce the workload considerably, while still maintaining the level of potential for impact.

Second, your spreadsheet will help you to maintain some discipline. It means that you do not have to keep thinking about what to do next and it breaks down the work into manageable chunks. This can often alleviate the mental pressure created by a long list of activities.

Lastly, depending on how senior you are and/or how much resource you have available, it may be possible to get help with implementing your plan.

The keys to success are regularity, consistency and focus. Even if you do one thing each week, it will get you somewhere.

Plan it in your diary once a week or every day – whatever best suits your routine. We all know that if you leave blank space in your diary, someone will fill it for you. You need to block out the time, just as you

Figure 2: Profile plan to complete

Activity plans	Months											
Online profiles												
Testimonials												
Contact building												
Friends and helpers – what can you do for people?												
Setting up meetings												
Titles/volunteering												
Awards												
Innovation reading and thinking time												
Posts												
Writing articles												
Contacting platforms to submit articles												
Vlogs/blogs												
Webinars/courses												
Speaking/presenting externally												
Partnerships												
Products												
Internal profile												
Personal progress reviews												

would for an important meeting. Prioritise yourself. It's not easy to think of this as being as important as other activities in your week. However, this will help to build your career in the long term and will enhance your day-to-day experiences and opportunities. Don't hold yourself back.

3. Establish a routine

Be consistent in terms of posting online and building followers. Even a mere five minutes each day will help. What you cannot do is jump in and out and then expect results. What you will find, gradually, is that the results you see will increase and gain momentum over time.

So, make a commitment to yourself and see it through.

"I had put off doing anything about my online presence because it seemed such a big task. When I realised it would be okay just to do five minutes a day, I completely changed my approach. I started to do it with my morning coffee and because I did it every day, it became easier to do, as I established a habit. After a couple of months, I started to see results. I had more followers and arranged a few meetings with new business contacts off the back of these new follows. Starting to produce articles and posts and ideas was an easy next step."

"I realised I wasn't achieving as much as I had hoped. I cut my plan right down and focused on it more. I began to feel I was succeeding rather than failing. I forgot the only judge of how I was doing was me."

TASK 24: Find the time

The best way to allocate time to promoting your profile is to put it in your diary as a weekly slot:

- Use five minutes in the morning with a coffee to make new connections and arrange chats and meetings with new contacts.
- Use a couple of lunch hours to think about posts and read articles that might inspire ideas and thoughts for innovation. Even having a chat with a friend or colleague can help you to innovate.
- Fridays are a good day to write articles.
- Essentially, you need to put aside time and have a plan that you can implement in that time. That way, it becomes a habit and you don't have to keep thinking about what to do next. You know where you are going.

Now block out the time in your diary...

XVIII. And finally...

1. So, what have we discovered?

- Potential clients will look for a number of different sources, as well as referrals, to confirm that you are to be trusted. We need to ensure that you and your profile are present wherever they look for that reassurance.
- Treat yourself in the same way as you would your firm. Develop your own objectives, target market, key messages and tone. Find your own USP and develop your own brand.
- Use a good-natured approach, combined with the psychological tools of reciprocity and association, to build relationships and open up new opportunities for yourself. Remember to say 'yes'.
- Use all of the different channels available to you that are relevant to your target market. If you write an article, use it in as many different places as possible. The more often people see you, the more they will know you and the more they will trust you.
- Keep your profile and material up to date. People do look and they will judge you and your professionalism. The competition is doing this, so don't fall behind.
- Keep building up your connections on social media so that you can engage with new and old contacts, start conversations and ask for meetings, as well as being able to promote what you are doing to them.

- Seek out opportunities to put yourself forward for awards, get involved in voluntary areas which will open doors and don't forget to ask for testimonials.
- Always get someone else to check what you are putting out publicly if you can't see any potential flaws yourself. Do this until you feel more confident about what you are doing. It will also help you to ensure that your material is interesting and the right length before you publish it.
- Whether you're speaking, writing or commenting, ensure that you are solving the problems of others. Focus on them rather than what you want to say, as this will generate far more interest. Your audience will identify with what you're saying. Always ask: "What's in it for them?"
- Finally, be committed. Make a plan and stick to it on a regular basis. Implementation is what makes the real difference and that is where others often fall down.

2. Get going!

Now it's down to you! You have the plan. You have your ideas. You know how to develop them and you have actions set out for the next year. As with everything, what you put into this, you will get out of it. Do not let a lack of self-belief or confidence get in the way of your personal career success. Other people don't, so why should you? You might surprise yourself...

TASK 25: Over to you...

Notes

1 Apple Dictionary.
2 https://spinsucks.com/entrepreneur/referral-marketing/.
3 *Ibid.*
4 Daniel Kahneman, *Thinking Fast and Slow* (Farrar, Straus and Giroux, 2013).
5 www.lexico.com/definition/thought_leadership.
6 www.forbes.com/sites/johnhall/2019/11/03/is-thought-leadership-everything-its-cracked-up-to-be/?sh=144955e29341.

About the author

Rebecca Harding
Communications, marketing and business development expert
Saltwhistle Communications
rebecca@saltwhistle.com

Rebecca Harding is a communications, marketing and business development specialist. She is the worldwide chairman of the Society of Women Writers and Journalists, and was recently awarded Highly Commended Finalist in the UK Institute of Directors' Non-executive Director of the Year award. She is a professional member of the Chartered Institute of Public Relations and is a retired vice chairman of the Chartered Institute of Marketing.

Rebecca founded Saltwhistle Communications in 2000 and has developed a portfolio of clients within the professional services industry. Clients range from multinational firms such as accountants Deloitte, PwC and EY to law firms such as Stephenson Harwood, Norton Rose Fulbright and Weightmans, as well as international businesses such as WPP's Mediacom, J Walter Thompson (now Wunderman Thompson) and Mindshare. Each client benefits from a range of services, including partner and board advisory services, digital and classic communications and marketing solutions, pitching and business development, and courses for professionals. Much of

Rebecca's current work is international and she works with firms to increase their international effectiveness, as well as helping to draw together their international tenders/pitches.

Prior to establishing Saltwhistle Communications, Rebecca was responsible for communications at Andersens. She also worked in marketing within the energy industry, with corporations such as BNFL, BP, ESSO and Shell. She appears on a chat show for the BBC and has been quoted and published widely in trade journals, as well as national newspapers such as the *Sunday Times*.

In her spare time, Rebecca has qualified as a yacht skipper and has trained as a game ranger in Kruger National Park, and as a falconer.

About Globe Law and Business

Globe Law and Business was established in 2005. From the very beginning, we set out to create law books which are sufficiently high level to be of real use to the experienced professional, yet still accessible and easy to navigate. Most of our authors are drawn from Magic Circle and other top commercial firms, both in the UK and internationally.

Our titles are carefully produced, with the utmost attention paid to editorial, design and production processes. We hope this results in high-quality publications that are easy to read and a pleasure to own. Our titles are also available as ebooks, which are compatible with most desktop, laptop and tablet devices. In 2018 we expanded our portfolio to include journals and Special Reports, available both digitally and in hard-copy format, and produced to the same high standards as our books.

We'd very much like to hear from you with your thoughts and ideas for improving what we offer. Please do feel free to email me at sian@globelawandbusiness.com with your views.

Sian O'Neill
Managing director
Globe Law and Business

www.globelawandbusiness.com

www.ingramcontent.com/pod-product-compliance
Ingram Content Group UK Ltd.
Pitfield, Milton Keynes, MK11 3LW, UK
UKHW060219140526
471061UK00005B/44

9 781787 423541